LIFE IN A BOAT SHELL

A Paddler's Collection Of Essays

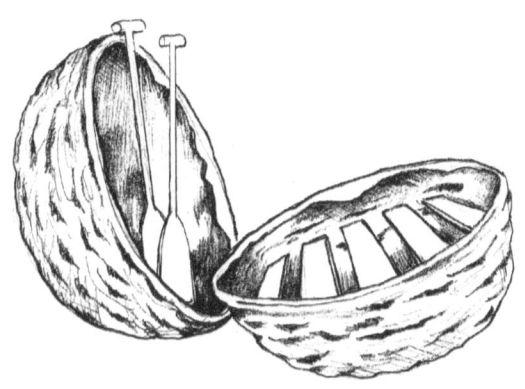

written and illustrated by
pinky manzano

Life In A Boat Shell copyright © 2020 by Pinky Manzano.

All rights reserved, including the right to reproduce this book or portions thereof in any form whatsoever. For information, address the publisher.

ISBN: 9798574818374

Pinky Manzano has no responsibility for the persistence or accuracy of URLs for external or third-party Internet Websites referred to in this publication and does not guarantee that any content on such Websites is, or will remain, accurate or appropriate.

Designations used by companies to distinguish their products are often claimed as trademarks. All brand names and product names used in this book and on its cover are trade names, service marks, trademarks and registered trademarks of their respective owners. The publishers and the book are not associated with any product or vendor mentioned in this book. None of the companies referenced within the book have endorsed the book.

Disclaimer: Portions of this book are works of nonfiction. Certain names and identifying characters have been changed.

Front and back cover design by the author

Printed in Manila, Philippines

First printing, 2020.

www.pinkymanzano.com

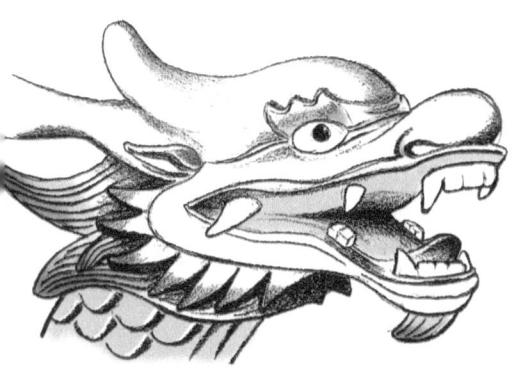

What's Inside...

Introduction 1

Discipline 4

Punctuality 10

Determination 16

Teamwork 22

Perseverance 28

Camaraderie 36

Final Thoughts 42

The Evolution of a Dragon Boat Paddler 46

Dragon Boat Glossary and Terms of Basic Commands 47

Acknowledgments 53

About the Author 55

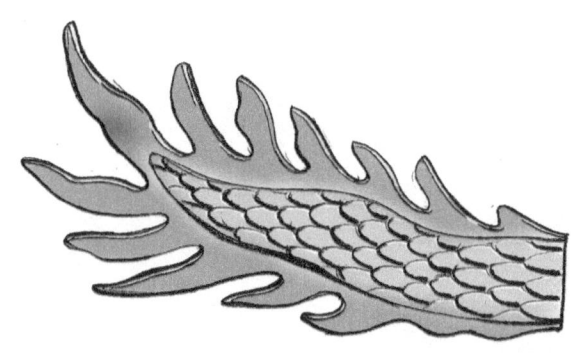

INTRODUCTION

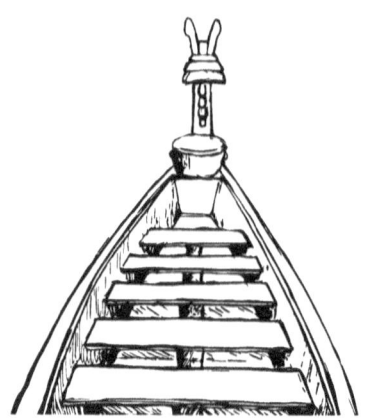

> *"There's only one way to avoid criticism:
> do nothing,
> say nothing,
> and be nothing."*
> **Aristotle**

Ten years ago, I returned to dragon boat training and reunited with the same sports team after an eighteen-year hiatus — initially hoping to adapt to a fitness regimen that would keep middle-aged people like us, to a degree, fit and healthy. What started as fun weekend training leveled up to more serious ones until it found us our first international race competition in Thailand and the rest is history. Okay, not the kind that puts us in the books but hey, we seriously rolled and raked in some golds, silvers, and bronze medals along the way, racing competitively in countries like Taiwan, South Korea, and Japan.

Taking on this journey opened up my eyes to the other life-long lessons that go beyond the victories and the physical aspect of the sport — the virtues that grow out of the practice and the benefits that help impact our character. Just as in any group or organization, conflicts always arise and these become sources of growth. We, as a team, had our share of good times, especially when rewarded for our achievements, the tangible things, numbers, and symbols that define us, but it is often the journey we set aside and take for granted. The small, even uneventful experiences in the process make us feel whole and complete in the end.

This effort is a sheer attempt to document some of my personal experiences gathered in my days as an active participant in the sport of dragon boat. While I am no writer, nor have I authored any type of prose in my life for public consumption, this collection of essays comes to simply gather my thoughts and ideas, recollecting my encounters, inspiration,

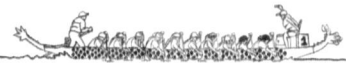

and little successes borne of the years spent as a paddler, experiencing it with a team and encapsulating life in what I call a "boat shell".

I hope this collection comes as an easy read especially made for those who are interested to know more about the sport, for those who have witnessed and are amazed at racing human-powered boats, as well as for those enthusiasts who have been "at bay" due to the coronavirus shutdown.

As a bonus, I took the effort of adding illustrations to this collection to visualize the scenes and add life to the pages, which was a pleasant opportunity for me to bring back to life a long-forgotten skill, the creativity I had long feared to be dead. I do hope you find the anecdotes interesting and they take you, hopeful paddlers, back to relive the spirit, and to the casual readers, learn the virtues that have brought paddlers like me alive in this sport.

Oars up!

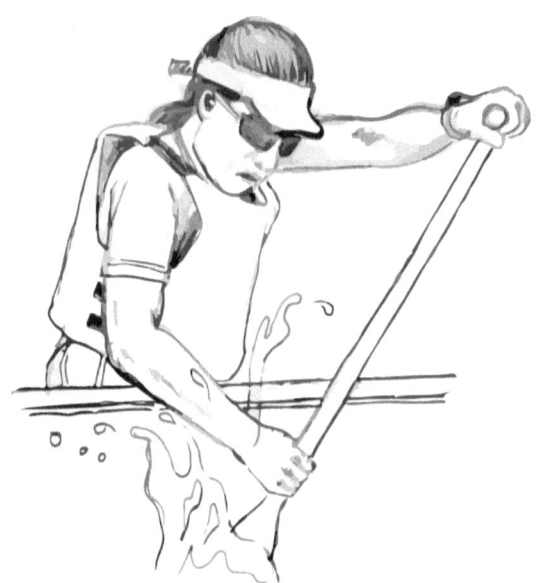

To move forward, we have to pull our load behind us.

DISCIPLINE

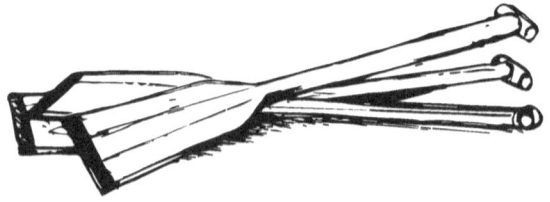

> *"When you arise in the morning, think of what a precious privilege it is to be alive – to breathe, to think, to enjoy, to love."*
> **Marcus Aurelius**

*I*t was a dark and brisk Saturday morning and I am jolted by the 4:30 a.m. rooster alarm. My bright pink rash guard, Speedo board shorts, and a white visor were neatly folded at the foot of my bed, the last thing I remember doing five hours ago before I set my morning alarm. The previous Saturdays had been routinely the same. With eyes still shut, I am conflicted curled up in a cozy bed, hardly believing that anyone could be up this early. I finally pulled myself up, particularly saw it more practical to grab the towel and purposely head straight to the shower. There was a strange intention of making things happen for that Saturday, the third weekend of training.

Our paddle orders would be arriving today, customized by a local supplier for less than the cost of a branded Grey Owl. Something new I knew the team was looking forward to. We had been using two-decade-old wooden oars, some borrowed and most beaten up through time, slightly heavier than a typical paddle. We had coined them dumbbell oars.

I drove a constant 80 kph along the highway and covered the 26 km stretch to the bay in a little over twenty minutes. Coach D was ready nearby the dock, easily recognizable in his famous green plaid board shorts, when about seven teammates, then ten more, made it to the coach's call time and people gathered in small groups. The team secretary listed down the usual delinquents in her brown clipboard. The void parking space was now filling with people finding their huddle as the grey skies gently turned pink and bright orange. The morning felt brighter and more alive.

A group of other paddlers waited, ready in their run-

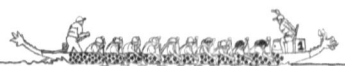

ning shoes at 5:30, while some hurriedly moved to change from flip-flops. The faint murmurs raised as more people arrived to check-in, exchanging high-fives and showing off new gear. You would hear chitchats going over the week's events, catching up on the humdrum of city living or musing on post-training breakfast.

Beginning that weekend, a tardy fine would be charged for attendance infractions. Coach D has made us aware of the conditions of the upcoming race and asked us to take the training seriously, reminding us to step up and maintain the discipline to keep up with the progression of the program. With the hopes to inspire, he usually amused us of his strong days paddling for the Navy and proudly recalls how in the intensity of races towards the last powerful strokes, he would already lift himself from his seat all the way to the finish line, a feat that was incredibly hard to do. What amazing core, I thought.

News this week was that the team's participation in the swan boat race in Thailand was just acknowledged and confirmed by the organizer. There was a slight apprehension with the way Coach D spoke and warned us about the event. The swan boat is a slight variation of the dragon boat and there were adjustments needed from our end. Beneath the excited faces, we could easily sense each other's qualms tucked somewhere, like clammy hands onstage saying memorized lines, half dead-as-ready and half knowing the lines.

This would be the first race in close to twenty years, the first time we would be in Thailand representing a team and having only the slightest idea of how the races went. Who were we vying with? How does the swan boat work? What are the conditions of the water in that river? How to use the paddle without the T-end? How strong are the other teams in the event? Whether we were after winning or simply taking our chances for the experience, we had to feel resolved with a common cause to help us fulfill being out there as a team.

We were undoubtedly seasoned paddlers, but our lame bodies from basic yoga stretching left us like sickly soldiers in battle at the end of practice. Some openly whined, while others were silent. Fifteen weeks to race day and our days were numbered. I presumed that each personally knew, or at least

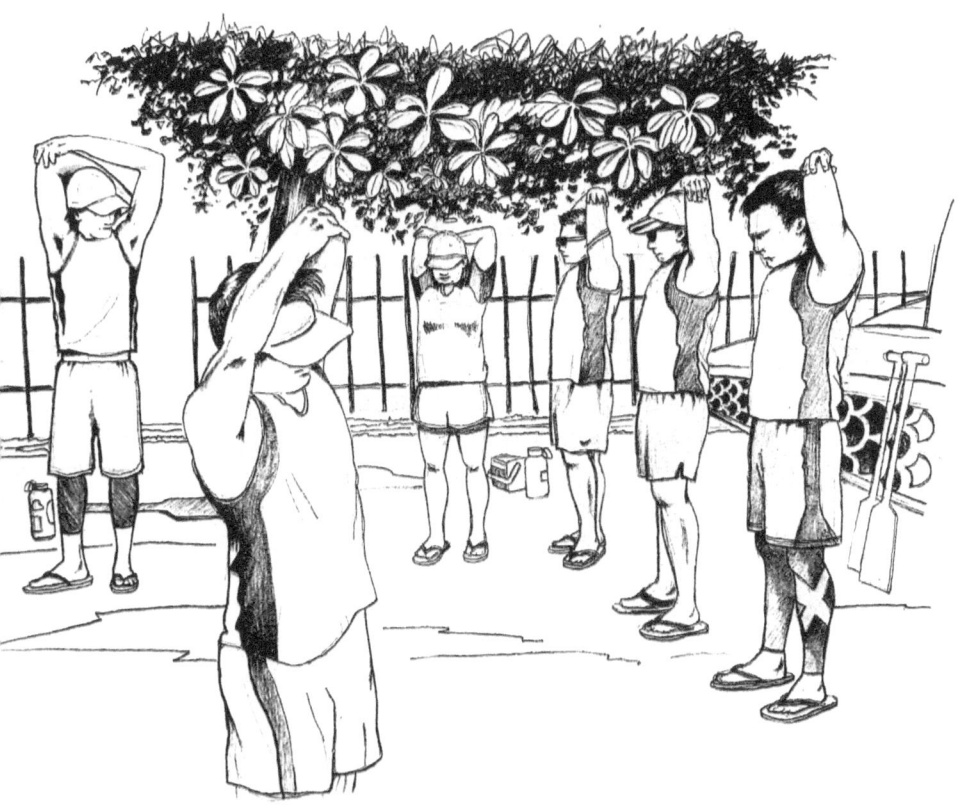

were honest enough to admit the tremendous amount of work we still had to work on. Many may have wondered how much of themselves can they commit, if at least conceivable, to the required schedules, to the pressures of training, to improving the mindset for physical endurance and sustaining it through the succeeding weeks.

Improvement is intentional and self-discipline is the key. We needed to open our minds to the journey being long and difficult. Our morning routine starts with a 15-min stretching program. Plastic training cones are set up on the pavement for strength-building relays, followed by 30-minute sprint workouts around the block in the parking grounds. By 6:30, we go for a one-hour boat training executing varying paddling exercises from the designed program of the day. After which, we are back for ground training with our yoga mats for post-training core exercises. We usually thought our ful-

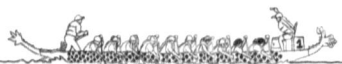

ly-packed morning activities seemed to have worked us up for the entire week and enough to keep us craving for a well-deserved team breakfast.

Most of us looked forward to the weekend training for the fun part of it, the established friendships among the team members, the nurturing community, and the entertaining tales tirelessly retold from the intense early rowing years. With stories and old photos revived, they brought us back to our lean, sinewy days when we did not even bother to check our heart rates. We hoped to still effortlessly do the same graceful paddling and perform in whatever age, shape, or size. Times have gone by and so was the stroke technique we came to know. What used to be just arm-strength training has now become a full-body workout.

Between lunges and side bend, our hamstring cried, and joints popped and cracked in the dead morning silence. "Ohh, Lord. I am now regretting the merlot and staying up late last night," one groaned between widely stretched legs and eight more counts in the humored jests of others. It is a challenging shift of lifestyle for most of us getting out of our routine where most are employed and professionals on top of having family roles to juggle. I was thankful to have started the running regimen three months before joining, thinking I could have somewhat gained an advantage.

Through the years, the local dragon boat community has grown to over forty teams, having started only with four teams when we learned the sport. Most are private club teams belonging to organizations, colleges, and different groups. But the competition was bigger and the age bracket more diversified, which upped the game of paddling as a sport. None of our seasoned skills would matter now, and there were lingering questions in everyone's minds. Am I ready to commit to this sport and this team? Am I ready for rigid physical and mental sessions? Am I ready to squeeze this into my already busy weekend schedule, to sacrifice a part of family time and other leisures?

Though the desire to gather all and reunite the members of the team was strong and apparent, our minds knew perfectly well, (and unfortunately with some dread) that whatever we were subjecting our physical bodies into would be challenging, long, and tiresome. A tedious and patient process of motivating oneself many times, mentally and physically preparing ourselves for training, following orders from the coach, respecting the program's goals and meeting the scheduled time, performing feats we are not sure we can still do, committing ourselves to up the game and cultivating a strong sense of discipline that inspires one another, maintaining restraint that helps us cross the finish line. This was the start of our journey towards developing the necessary discipline.

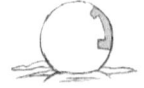

PUNCTUALITY

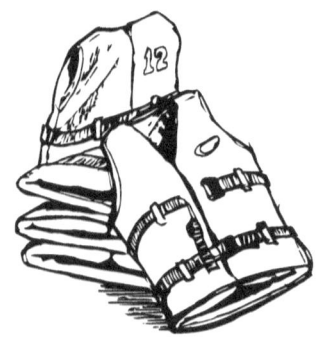

> *"Better three hours too soon than a minute too late."*
> **William Shakespeare**

Living ten short blocks away from my high school, I had a terrible reputation for being late, that I would run out of excuses for tardiness slips. We were a brood of four sisters that shared a ride in the morning, and the school registrar already knew us too well; she would refer to all of us by our last name. I am not certain as to why we would always run late, but we all shared the same notion that the proximity was relative to getting to school on time, at least in time to catch the final bell ring. But learning its value was a habit I eventually parted with as I grew older or until I had to face it myself later on as a mother dealing with kids or as a front-runner leading my own team at work.

Joining the club as weekend warriors meant there had to be trade-offs. No more late-night Friday side trips for dinners, coffee, alcohol bingeing, and extended socials. Working full time holding an office job in a fast-paced marketing and retail industry, I looked forward to that final day in the week where we could relax and cap off the busy week on a Friday night. With the majority of the senior paddlers fitting the same age group, status, and professional environment, we were basically going through the same scenario accepting the consequence of our compromise.

One Friday night, I am returning from a three-day business overseas trip close to midnight. My mind ruminates on gears, hydration, and physical preparedness for the next few hours until daybreak. Five weeks into physical weekend training, my body had gotten used to the routine. A gleaming sense of commitment somehow surfaced, and I wanted to

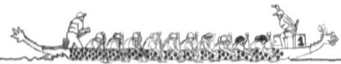

show up at the bay earlier and felt more energized than I could remember.

Coach D gave us a rundown of the new program. The workout program would be extended with increased sets and reps, and we had to prepare for time-trials. We had a mini health station that day after training to check and take down our individual stats, blood pressure, height and weight for body fat and mass index to discover who needed the weight-loss program. Coach D figured we needed to work heavily on our cardio and introduced us to the Indian run that summer. We jogged in single file, and the last person sprints to the front, which we did repeatedly during those hot and humid summer days. Very tiring cardio workout, and I can only guess those who were still out of shape were probably cursing their way through the sprints.

Towards the sixth week of training, the headcount dwindled down to half a boat. A week has passed after the Easter holidays, down to seven pairs, then five. Coach D felt disappointed as we huddled. We had improved in five weeks, bringing down our lap time by three to four seconds every week, and he reminded everyone not to put all that effort to waste by missing out or turning up late for practice. I wished I had shared the kind of motivation I felt earlier, even with a lack of rest and sleep with the rest of the team. It was not as much fun when the numbers went down and the work grew harder. When people got hungover from the holidays, we always slid back to where we started.

During the post-training discussion, the focus was on the punctuality of some members, and while the fines were helping us gain on the financial side, the team was sacrificing unbalanced training, and the waning dedication did not cultivate a positive outlook on the team. With the race coming up, we could not afford to take the slack.

We were expected to show up three days a week, follow the program, and respect the time and schedule, most especially of those who painstakingly show up consistently every morning during practice. Showing up for practice played 50% of the decision to earn a seat in the race line up. "Your timely attendance is an indication of your interest and commitment for the upcoming race", Coach D reminded. "Please show consideration for those who are meeting the schedule and spending valuable time working hard," another teammate who never missed practice chimed in.

Let's face it, five or ten minutes late would not mean a lot to put one far behind, but it unconsciously diffused the interest of others and brought the team's energy lower. For those who waited or burned more training hours, it seemed of little value to be getting ahead of the group and gaining indi-

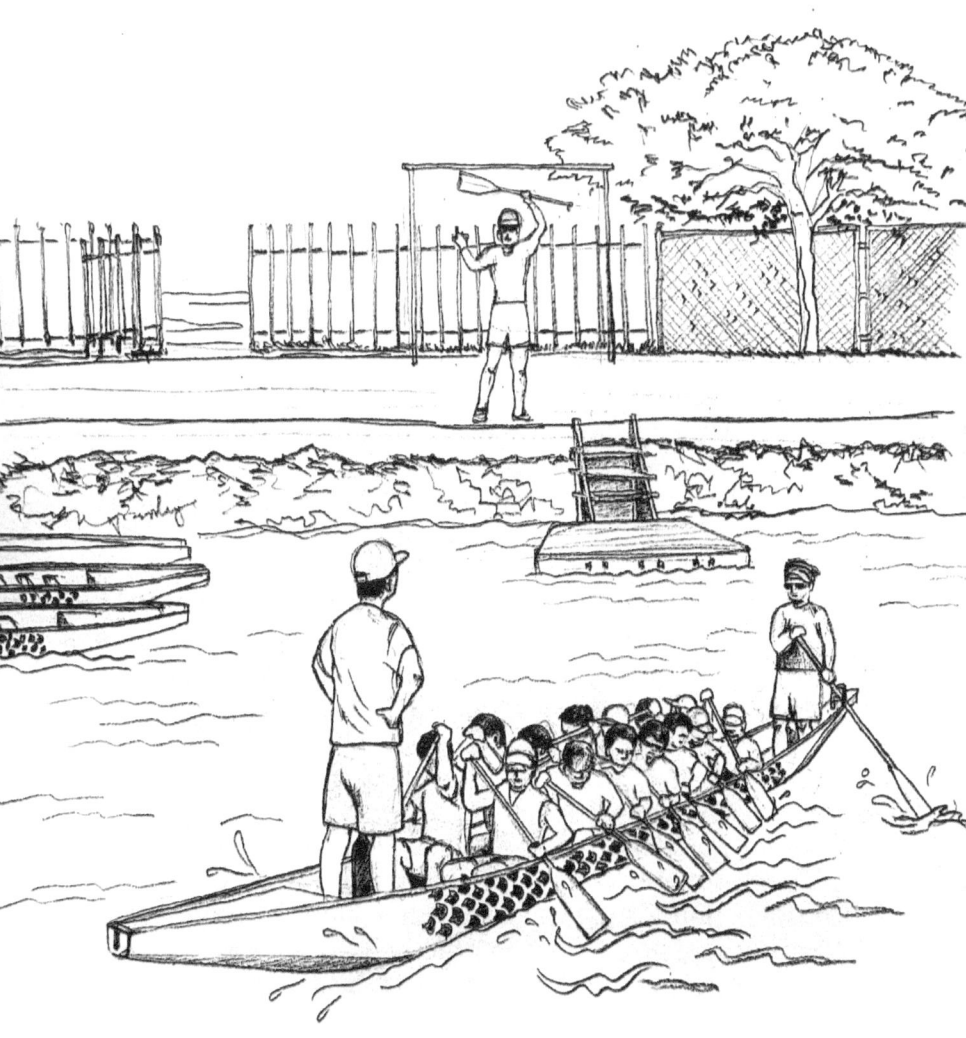

Punctuality

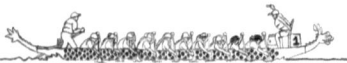

vidual results. This risks gradually losing interest in the team and settling mostly on self-improvement, losing the essence of what dragon boat is all about: teamwork and harmony.

There are those who struggle with being on time despite their best efforts or there are those who are habitual latecomers. Their feeble attempt to catch up usually ends up short and they desperately provide an assortment of reasons for not making it on time. At a basic level, being punctual is a sign of consideration and respect for other people's time and, in this case, the team's commitment. If this continues to be violated, it often eventually affects the way the team behaves and performs for the long term.

We have this teammate known to be habitually late and on some weeks, he would flit in and out of practice. Sometimes he would show up right when we had just taken off from the dock or he would just conveniently show up in time for team breakfast. He had been fined repeatedly and he was behind his dues.

On this particular day, he wanted to stress a point and must have been bothered by not being able to meet the time despite his efforts. After we had docked and readied ourselves with our yoga mats, he kept insisting to adjust the attendance policies and lower the fines.

"I was only a few minutes late and was out at the dock," he argued in vain. "I do regular gym time and work just as hard..." he added, knowing it would risk his seat in the boat.

From a practical viewpoint, attendance fines have become an opportunity to augment the funding for the team. This will help us cover some of our expenses for the upcoming race event. While this teammate's strength and physical capabilities put him in advantage, he would have to realize that his attitude and respect for the policies and goals of the team puts more value on his role.

I would like to think that time is linked to respect and that punctuality stems from respect. Being on time shows consideration for other people's time and effort, and if this basic form of respect is compromised, it can create feelings of doubt and may considerably affect the dynamics of a team in the long run. As in the case of the dwindling of paddlers before and until after the Easter holidays, this is attributed to some members offhandedly committing the tardy card.

I belong to a society where lateness (embarrassingly) has become close to innate as a culture. Where a few minutes late has become acceptable or the traffic excuse becomes a convenient topic to open meetings or discussions. However, this is one practice that is adaptable and can be easily improved by cultivating good habits. The simple act of showing up early silently communicates with our peers that we take them, their business, ourselves, and our business seriously.

In our world now that real-time communication tools, video calls, online meetings et al., replace face-to-face meetings, the convenience of technology helps us meet this essential virtue. But as we slowly move back into the normal, I hope this becomes a habit we take with us seriously.

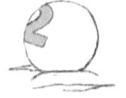

DETERMINATION

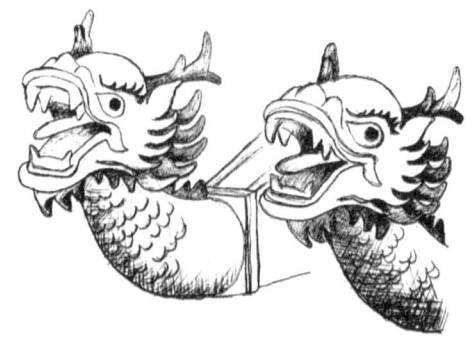

> *"It does not matter how slowly you go so long as you do not stop."*
> **Confucius**

The loud bullhorn went off. An Asian man, perhaps Chinese, is heard from the opposite end of the lake where the event marshalls responsible for the boats at the starting point were stationed, "Are you ready!" It was not even a question but a stern warning that another heat was about to begin. The blank pistol is fired to start the heat and oar blades angrily dig deep into the water. Paddlers lunge forward, reaching as far as their oars can go, racing every inch through the water with three other contenders.

Meanwhile, boat number one lightly paddled away from the loading dock and headed towards the starting area. Ten pairs of paddlers, our own steersman, and a drummer who sat across two seats away from me were on its way to the starting point where teams were asked to queue for the next heat. We wanted to witness the ongoing race until they reached the 500-meter mark, but all were distracted. We wore our serious faces and gave a nervous smile since deep inside, we were jumpy and our hearts pounded harder than the drummer's beats. We spoke softly in the hulls, secretly calming ourselves, tugged the water bottles for a few gulps between small talk and silly jokes to wheedle our way out of the jitters. No matter how often we had raced, heading to the start line as we prepared for a new heat was always a nerve-racking moment. And in these quick moments of doubt, I reverse the psyche, by telling myself I had been wanting and waiting for this opportunity, a chance to showcase what we have been working for in the past months.

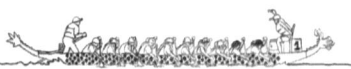

"Row.... Row...," the drummer called out in-between drum beats. He had a faint smile that told me his heart pounded as hard as ours. He clung to his seat as he bobbed forward from the rocking boat. He looked out into the water, carefully reading the signals of the marshalls. We trusted him as our eyes to guide us throughout the racecourse, past the buoys while he checked the opponents and watched out for other possible episodes along the race route that led us to the finish line. He reminds us again to keep our wandering eyes on the boat. All our attention and ears were aimed at the drummer's signals while we focused on every single stroke and watched as our blades rhythmically disappear through the water. Even a quick look at the opponents will cost us a fraction of a second. His role was important to keep us composed throughout the end of the heat.

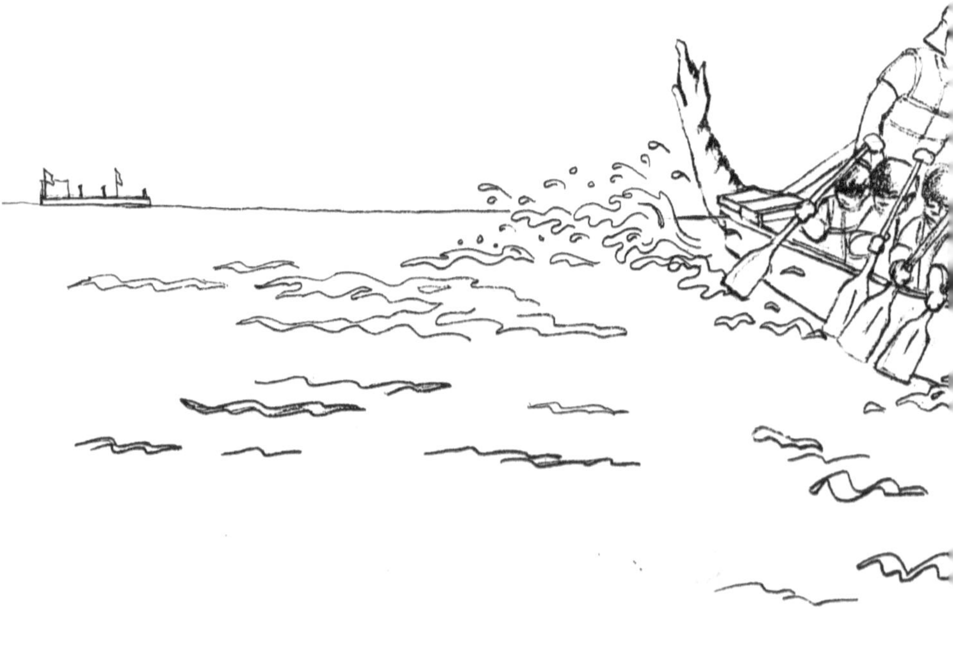

He glanced at the steersman to signal directions and to control the boat to its position. We paddled in and out, forward and backward until the steersman finally holds us in place in our designated lane number. Three more boats were adjusting their positions and we discreetly glanced at the colors and markings on their jerseys, stealthily sizing them up by the built of their bodies and the way they wore their game faces. As a way not to expose our tactics, the drummer uses our mother tongue to remind us to focus and keep our eyes inside the boat while giving directions.

He spoke quickly and strongly. Others stole a few moments to hydrate while some passed the drummer's messages to the back. The time finally came for the longest two minutes of our lives.

The voice-over spoke in Mandarin and somewhere between the inaudible words, we had to be alert for signaling words like READY and GO. We securely planted ourselves in position, legs and feet firmly settled, paddles flat on the gunwale, one hand firmly on the tee and the other loosely gripping the end of the shaft. The marshall throws a line to each boat and the drummer secures it until the starting pistol goes off. The winds and currents constantly nudged us too often, while pacers and tail-ends either pushed or pulled the water

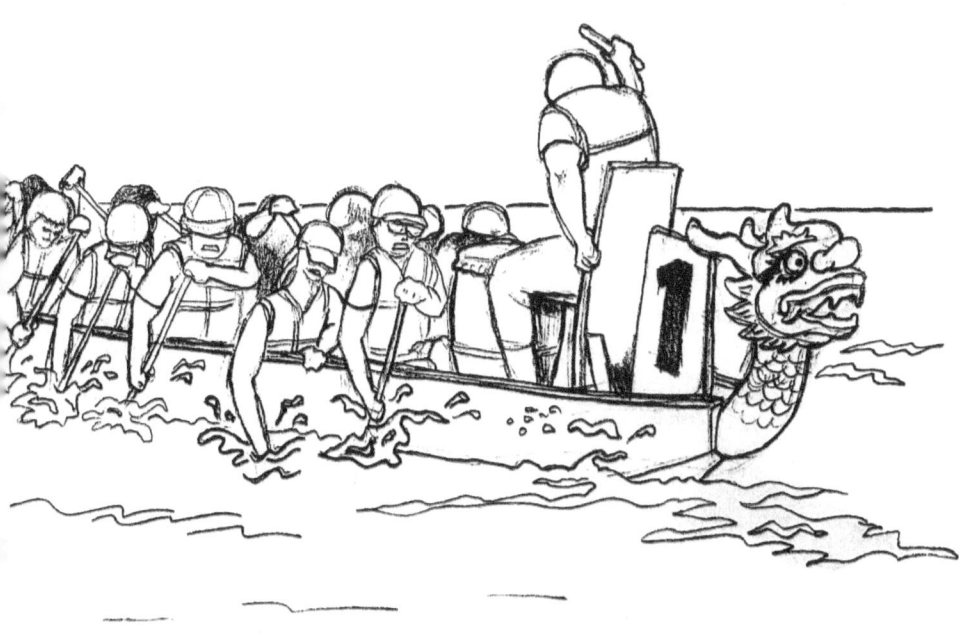

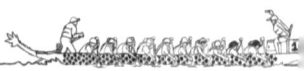

to hold us in place. Now all were still.

Finally, we heard the pistol fire, the drummer releases and hurls the line away from the boat and towards the dock. I slice the paddle into the water for the first time. "Ready for thirty! Row!" The line floated alongside the hull, creating a loop right where I was aiming to dig in for the second stroke. The blade plunges through the water, but the line caught the oar by the wide end of the blade and sends me thrown backward, hitting the bottom board between the paddler's legs, where I am immediately pulled up and pushed back to my seat. The length of the oar disappeared in the blue and white bubbly spray, quickly slipping from my hand until I realized that I literally lost the oar. The force of the moving boat rocked hard back and forth and constantly swelled forward. Nobody spoke, but the drummer, "Roooow!" His angry bellow was aimed at me. Even with a spare oar in the boat, there was not a single second to waste. Grunts and growls and angry cries rose from within like muffled sounds.

Frustrated, angry, and rendered useless, I firmly gripped onto the gunwale, now barefoot since my flip flops had drifted away somewhere, I reached forward and paddled with my bare hand catching up with the rapid strokes of the first thirty. I let out a blusterous scream with the drummer, "Rooow!" I stormed a swinging arm and plunged it deeply enough in unison with the rest of the blades, I continued to pull as much water with an empty open and raging palm. All the balked energy now shifted to ruthless rowing as my legs shivered and body jerked forward. I would not have the crew carry my weight throughout the heat and far more ridiculous now to be jumping off the boat and thinking, how can I be not so ready for this!

My head spun and adrenaline kicked in as we continued to paddle harder. It was a failed attempt at using the oar and an uncanny way of showing support to the nineteen others pulling the boat. I am left with no choice and I needed to help the team.

The drummer calls for the last kick, the final 40 or 50 strokes. "Ready for last kick! Pick up, pick up...!" I became fully aware of how the force was so strong that I admired how the team moved the boat. For the final call past the last few orange-colored buoys towards the finish line, I found myself heels up and knees down as we screamed towards the finish.

We let out a loud scream of relief at the finish line. Strong high fives in the air, hard jabs on each other's floaters, which later on were called PFD's as personal floating devices, cries of relief and sighs of satisfaction are heard. Everyone cheered me on with each still trying to wrap their heads around the open palm paddling. I recall feeling frustrated awhile back but accidents are inevitable and I just felt thankful for not having been thrown off the boat with such strong force. The passion instinctively pushed me to thrust through the water with my bare hand to continue with the job expected of me.

It was finally over and while all were relieved, I wondered for a moment how I had reacted initially to the embarrassing fate. I was more composed now to accept and embrace without regrets. Nobody is ever prepared for such moments. It was necessary to think quickly and react well. I could not have done so without the determination we have naturally fostered through months of hard work.

Ironically at times, when faced with fear or discouragement or when we are not prepared for things and our expectations are not met, that is when we are put to the test and given a chance to show our persistence, courage, and grit. The ability to stay strong, committed and determined in the face of challenges and difficult situations. Often, we are discouraged by small letdowns, not realizing that it is the only way for us to grow stronger.

That heat placed us in second place and I was glad that despite the mishap, I was instinctively prepared to help and give them "a hand".

Teamwork

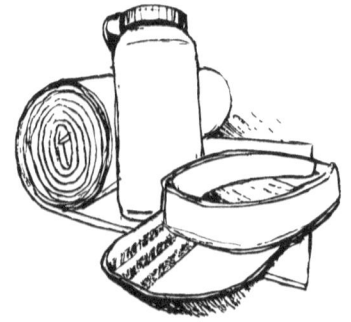

*"To go fast, go alone.
To go far, go together."*
African proverb

*F*or anybody who has closely witnessed a dragon boat competition, it is easy to see when one or many oars are not in unison with the movement of the boat. The momentum of the drift wanes or in a more disastrous case, the paddles collide and a string of unsequenced strokes happen or, worse, cause a boat to overturn. Dragon boat, when done right, is a perfect and clear demonstration of teamwork where the results are immediately seen. Everyone works in harmony to propel a boat, and when it is successfully done, the vessel moves swiftly and the strokes produce more efficiently with less pressure. Imagine how much more powerful it can be when all paddlers have the same mindset and attitude and the team exerts the optimal effort from start to finish. The concept of synchronized paddling is synonymous with teamwork, which is why I find dragon boat a challenging sport. No one member can be strong alone.

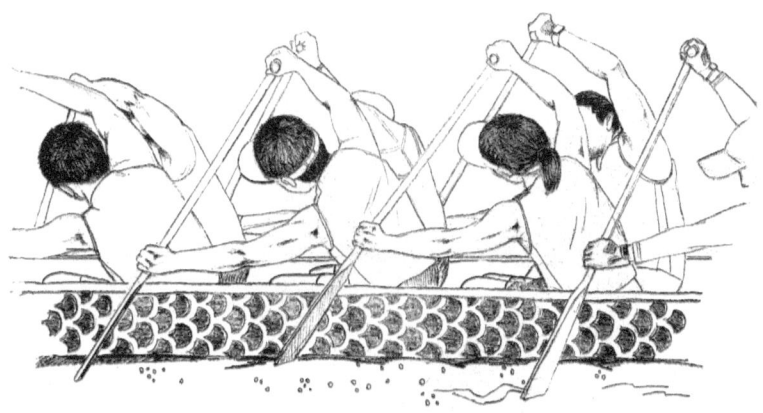

Teamwork

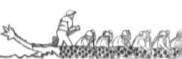

There is also this one part of the sport where an exhibit of teamwork is expressed. This happens when preparing for a race event.

One morning, after wrapping up all the physical agenda from training, we all gathered in a huddle and started the discussion looking at the long list of things to do as we counted the remaining weeks until the race date.

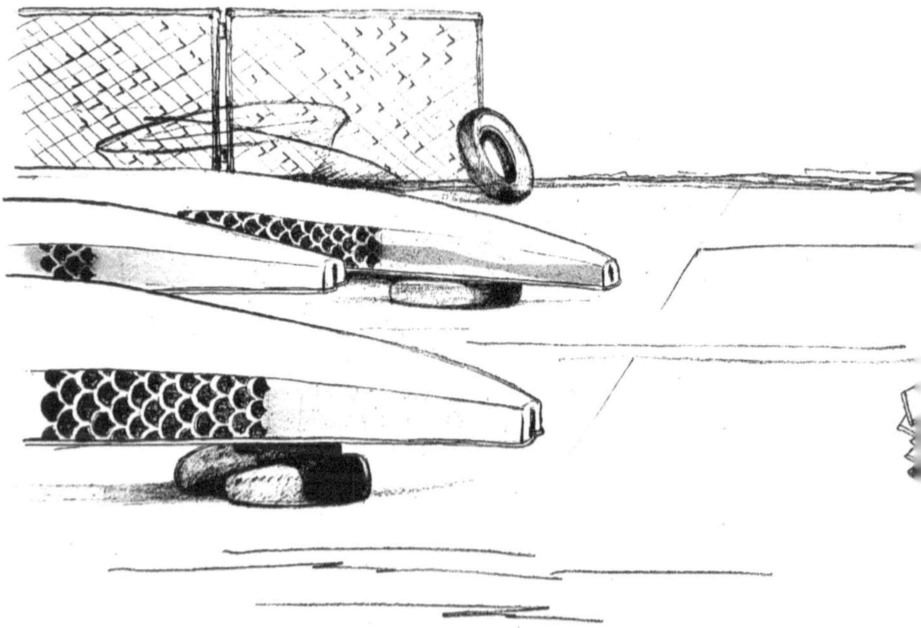

The team secretary brought her clipboard and clear folder of which held the many tasks we had to complete before booking our air tickets that week. We greatly depended on her since she held all our records and I often wondered where she was getting the time and energy performing in the boat as much as she laid effort in the administrative work for the team. She paid a tremendous amount of time and attention to coordinating the many aspects of managing the needs of the team, which she has been doing for quite some time now. She is up to date on attendance lists, physical stats, financial statements, race schedules, the team's passport details, correspondence with different local and international groups and offices, and so on. She always willingly did the job for the team given her nurturing nature.

For a party of 28 to 30 participants, preparing for an international event can be tasking and challenging. The team officers usually took care of one too many tasks until it gets daunting. So, to keep the entire process more organized, one of us prepared a set of committees and considered all tasks down to the most trivial, providing all the activities needed to be done in an orderly manner.

There was a committee on marketing for sponsorship, promoting the team to potential organizations interested to support the sport. This helps raise the needed funds

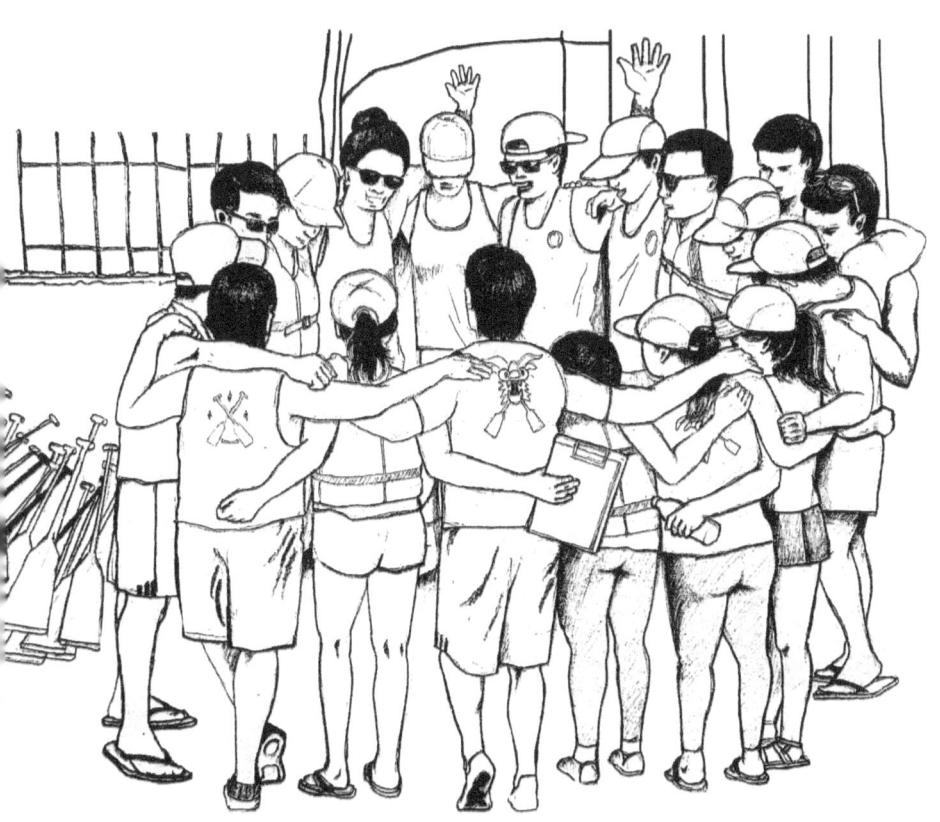

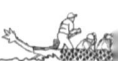

to determine whether we could shoulder Coach D's expense, among many other costs to consider. A committee was placed in charge of liaising with the local sports commission and the dragon boat federation for endorsement, permits, and travel tax refund documentation. There was a logistics committee responsible for the safekeeping and storage of our gears throughout our travel.

Many more committees were set up to address on-ground tasks — race schedule coordination, souvenirs and tokens (because we are courteous and gracious participants), guest relations — spokespersons tasked to meet with ambassadors, key persons and embassy personnel, the well-being of team members (composed of the team nurse and doctor), first-aid and medication, headcount, food-and-meals, flag, and banners (for safekeeping and hoisting of the national flag and positioning of our team banners), games and entertainment (for lull times during long event breaks in between heats), spiritual matters (a prayer leader to inspire us during tough moments), trash management and disposal, liquor supply (a party after the race is a must), lost and found, valuables and bag security. We even got someone as a sleep barker!

As it turned out, there were many ways, entertaining and interesting means to contribute to the team. Each member, even the silent ones we hardly heard speak, willingly volunteered. The discussion grew, and many started to chip in as more ideas came up. There were exchanges of emails, numbers chats, and laughter until the huddle was over. Afterward, many had dispersed to either take a shower or quickly change to dry clothes and went straight to the breakfast meeting.

Since I had access to suppliers, I volunteered to be in the uniforms committee, a team of one with extended help from someone who put together the material I needed to bring to the printer. Since I had access to suppliers who would customize, I volunteered to take the task. Three days before our scheduled flight, I would still haul the goods from the supplier, stuffing bags of uniforms in my hatchback, sorting sizes, gathering them in sets, labeling and distributing them individually at the airport, and as soon as we arrived

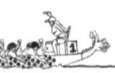

at the hotel. People always looked forward to receiving their uniform sets because it looked cool to show off and swap sports jerseys with the other club teams when the event ended.

Anybody belonging to a group can consider himself to be part of a team — a choice to be either a team member or a team player. Becoming a team player by extending help and support to a group offers more opportunities that can bring the team closer together. If each shares the right intentions and trusts each other to accomplish the work, a group of people can do more remarkable things than they can imagine.

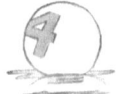

PERSEVERANCE

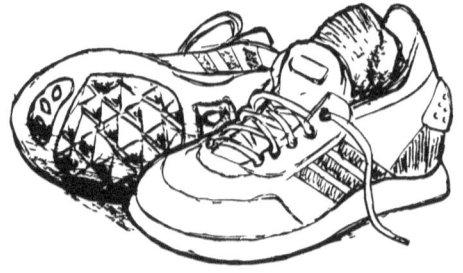

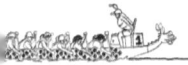

> *"Difficulties strengthen the mind,*
> *as labor does the body"*
> **Seneca**

Thailand was the first international race destination for the team after many years since we competed in Hongkong and Taipei back in the nineties. The experience promised to be different as we came across the invite "Thailand Swan Boat Festival". I imagined the long and narrow traditional boats unique to Thai culture, with a length good enough to fit up to 60 paddlers, 30 side-by-side rowing across the river. Many international teams from the Pacific came and many communities throughout the region looked forward to being part of this celebration at the Chao Phraya river. It felt like our local town fiesta.

That morning, I had slept only four and a half hours, catching the late-night flight out to Bangkok. Another hour and a half by bus until we reached the city hotel where I am bunking in with a cousin. She had flown in a day earlier to join the group for a leisurely tour of the city. She had been with the team as my recruit since our younger years when I would drag her with me to the bay whenever she slept over in our place for the weekend. Just like the rest of the team, she had her apprehensions about competing, more so as a first-timer internationally.

I had missed their bizarre food adventures in the market. The sweet durian, fried crispy silkworms, and grasshoppers, coconut milk sorbet served in cracked coconut husks, kway teow noodles in banana leaf, a variety of flavored sticky rice, and many others that I had hoped to experience in the next days after the race was over. The organizers will be taking us around the Bang Sai Royal Folk Arts Center for some pictorials with the team and the riverside food stalls abound where they would be available. Most of all, we would be seeing the beautiful river for the first time and experience being a part of the festival.

Four months earlier, this team of thirty and forty-year-olds did not even think they would be competitively racing again. We had little expectations gathering at the bay once a week for leisurely rowing. We went for simple wins of progress to justify a well-spent weekend fitness routine. Living out our paddler experiences again, stepping down the dock where we shrieked at crawling sea roaches, plunging through small patches of oil spills, rowing in the bay as if not a day passed since we last touched the rancid waters of the city bay. Until that morning, hundreds of miles away from home, we felt lucky, excited, and energized for practice day.

Looking our regular best in printed heather grey cotton

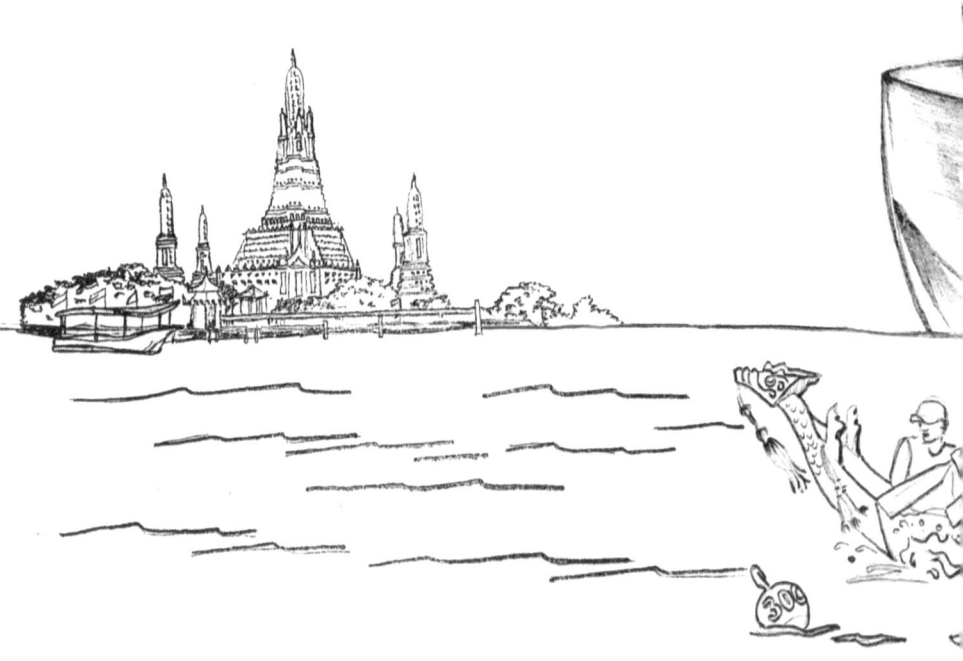

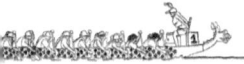

round neck shirts and cheap black athletic shorts, we showed up at the race site for practice at 6:30 that morning. Only two or three teams were out in the water. We surveyed the race site, walked the length of the course, followed the buoy markers, and sighed at what seemed to be the longest 650 meters we had ever seen. The team captain gathered us to the side of the dock for warm-up. Amidst the groans and lunges, a loud shriek of laughter breaks the silence after one of us had ripped open our China-made shorts. There goes our day one uniform and couldn't even be more looking forward to our better-looking racing jerseys tomorrow morning.

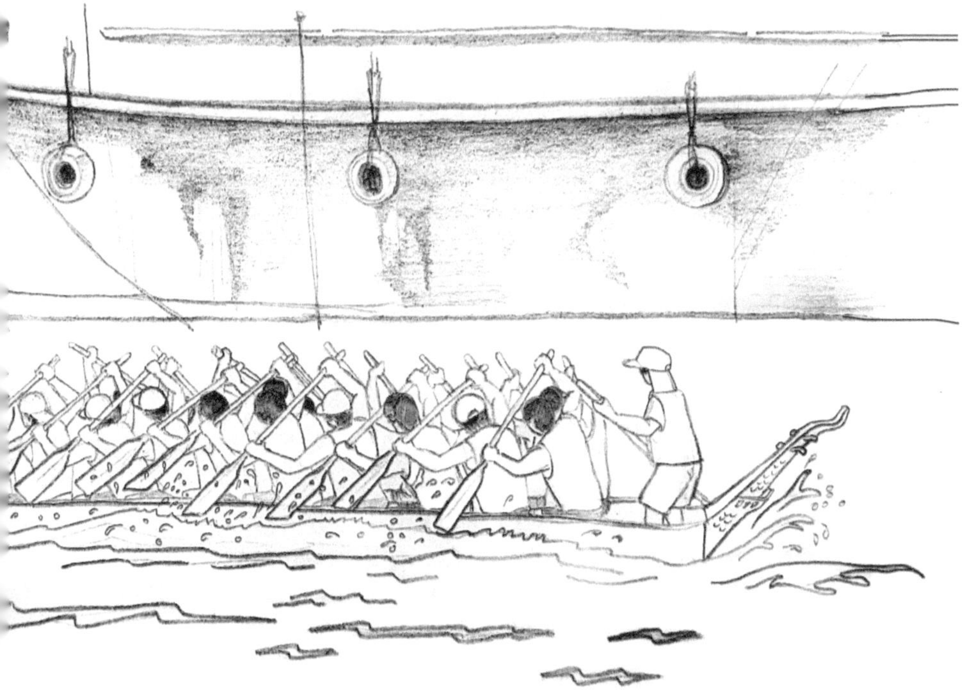

As soon as we loaded onto the boat, we carefully balanced our way to find our seats and inspected the unusual long paddles that had no grip. We noticed how the vessel differed from the dragon boat as the swan boat's head was of carved dark wood adorned with golden sparkling threads and colorful tassels. The river's undercurrent was silent but strong, and the water, full and dense. The long and narrow boat floated barely a palm's height above the surface of the water and its round hull made us hang on to the gunwales. There were no safety jackets or PFD's (personal floating device) provided, but Coach D made sure to include safety measures as part of the training. We only had to be evenly steady to keep the boat stable.

It was only practice day, but Coach D gave us a serious look in the boat. "Oars on the side!" he cried as he firmly held on to the paddle to balance himself as he watched us loading the boat. We spent an hour's training, marveled at the river and the bright Bang Sai structure on the side, imagining how the race was going to turn out tomorrow.

Race day came, the organizer's camera crew moved from one tent to the next interviewing teams that came from many places while prominent-looking guests continued to fill the stage where the ceremonies would be held. Later on, the event formally opened the official race with the iconic ancient Thai music of xylophones, drums, and gong chimes.

We were finally given our queue to be ready at the assembly area. Coach D was directing the line-up and ordered me to take the stroke and right-side pacer, a first-time for me. Dave sat ahead of me to pace for the left side, barely a foot away from where he can take the coach's roaring. My sweaty palms in half gloves inspect and grip the fairly long paddle. I looked straight ahead to see the fuzzy last buoy, now a tiny speck of white — the only thing my eyes will be aiming at in case I was tempted to look out of the boat. The massive barge allotted halfway down the course would be a good marker.

Coach D, together with the team captain, had thoughtfully worked the distribution in the boat, carefully considering each paddler's strength, attitude, mental, and body mass. The first four front pacers are usually light to average weight and must be able to start the motion of the boat by setting the right pace for each call. They are the "first" to serve the drummer's signal and must be cheerfully strong. I felt pressured to take the pacer's seat for the first heat of the day, but I did not hesitate. If I was going to challenge myself, this was an opportunity, a little discomfort should bring me some good, I openly

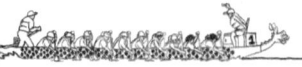

thought to myself.

Rows 4 to 8 are considered the middle section or the engine room and they possess average to excellent strength. It's an advantage for them to have closer access to the water where the output is maximized.

The last two pairs of paddlers towards the tail end are called the rockets of the boat. Similar to the front pacers, they should be light to average weight and should readily assist the steersman. They work like jet engines by pushing the boat forward. Being at the tail's end, they will always find the water hard and heavy and adjust their strokes and body position to assist the steersman.

We were the first to take our position at the start line and had to take a few adjustments, pacers and rockets rowing in and out to straighten the boat and fight the current while we waited for two more boats to slowly ease into the lanes.

Now all the boats remained silent and ready as the blank pistol fired. We braced for the first fifty strokes and shift to long strokes. The first sets of ten were heart-stopping, I gasped to catch my breath upon recovery. It was early to think of the barge, I thought.

"Slice deh wiiind," Coach D is tense, his jugular vein throbbing as he called out. "Ready for longs... one-zeroh," he calls out to signal 10 strokes. It would take many more sets of ten to reach the barge, the counts are tensely slow. I am consciously pacing the strokes and focusing on the water, many things are running in my head as we silently paddle in a gripping moment that feels like forever. The water sprays hard from a few inches away, crashing against the blades of the oars, and our squinted faces. The more we pushed and pulled the boat, the more water gushed in and out. On one hand, all the forceful motion threatened to flood more water into the boat, so the engine room seemed to be cautiously pulling the strokes away from the gunwale.

A quick moment of relief came through me as I saw the barge in the corner of my peripheral, like a slow dramatic panning scene in a movie. We were halfway and Coach D was still yelling the signals while two boats were gaining on us. The mounting lactic acid was gradually wearing out my arms and shoulders. "Breathe," I panted to remind myself.

"Rooowww!" Coach D screamed, prompting us that we had gone halfway. In a few moments, he calls out for the last kick, and a sudden tug jerks us forward, but I do not see the familiar white buoy. We kept going, paddling in a rhythmic pattern, feeling our blades slice the current together, swinging and digging. A few seconds later, another call for the last kick comes, and the strokes accelerate and nudges the boat forward. "But we are barely close to the final buoys," I thought to myself. The boat was weighing down and getting heavier by each stroke. We paddle angrily and gasp for more air, trying to recover from the long strokes and wait for what seemed endless.

Coach D calls out again, and hopefully, it is the final of the last kick. My face is drenched, my sunglasses have fogged, and my arms seem to have bailed out on me. I am tired, spent and my lips turned dry but pushed a little more one solid and unyielding stroke at a time. Finally, the white round speck is right before me, and I am alive, limp, and pale-faced. I hear screaming and excited cries of sheer relief. I turned around and some boats were ahead. We gladly raised our oars, exchanged hard high-fives in the air, and firm pats on the back. A group of relentless ex-paddlers who once thought they were out of shape to be competing again, out in the foreign open river, raging with spunk and nerve-racking spirit, we ruled the waters of Chao Phraya at that moment. We had finished our first 650-meter heat despite being behind in the racecourse by one boat's length. It did not matter. Not one of us stopped as we kept pushing and rowing until the end. All persevered to do what had to be done. We went against professional paddlers from two national teams in the open event and finished strongly towards the end, as winners in our own right. Everyone in the boat was glad we had all done it together, to have lived and experienced the moment we had long waited for.

Back in the tent, Coach D and the team captain gathered all for a huddle. We were lauded by the coach for how quickly we reacted to his signals and transitioned smoothly from the starts. Though he noticed that we were not able to maximize the recovery breathing at the exits, which caused some to slow down in between the last calls and be fully drained at the end of the race.

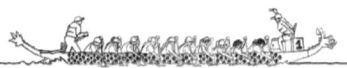

He apologized for prematurely calling out the signals of the last kick and regretted miscalculating the remaining last meters hoping to close in with the last boat towards the last hundred meters.

In summary, it was a good finish that impressed Coach D, especially for the first heat of the day, and the fact that we were not that far behind from the two strong national teams gave us a fairly good start.

Reaching the end of the line was not about winning. It was proof that as a team, we can do things together and with the right attitude, knowing we had struggled to be constantly better in months of practice, the persistence to improve, master the skill, being open to learning the new techniques and having been given the opportunity to show what we can do gave us all the satisfaction. The joy came from the quality of work we have expressed in that race, never giving up until we finished the job. The defining moment did not come from being first in a race but being able to complete and go through the journey, knowing that all did not stop and believed in one another.

Camaraderie

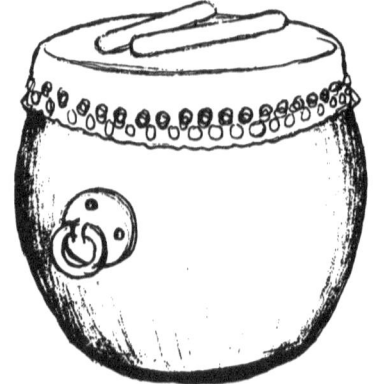

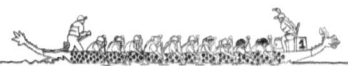

> *"Camaraderie doesn't happen by accident; developing a strong sense of trust, accountability, and togetherness around team goals requires intentional effort."*
> **Don Yaeger**

*C*amaraderie is one of those team qualities most often taken lightly and passively accepted as a virtue and is expected to grow naturally, particularly over time when a group or team is formed. When individuals are grouped and joined, even with a common goal in mind, we expect that people of different natures, personalities, temperaments, upbringing, and opinions to generally fall in place or simply take it from there to work, get along and function harmoniously. Camaraderie is more deliberate than essential, but likewise, just like any of the virtues I have pointed out in the other chapters, it requires a concerted effort for team members to reach a point of good rapport and warm, lighthearted friendship.

If there is one precious thing I have gained throughout my dragon boat experience, it is the friendship and family that has developed out of the time spent with people working and training in this sport, who in all other clubs would simply be called "teammates" or fellow members. Paddlers who know each other's strengths and weaknesses, do not think twice and can work productively, who are easily dependable to do the tasks because they know what each other is thinking and know one another well enough to function more effectively. This camaraderie extends from life in the bay and weekly training to sharing family milestones over coffee and supporting one another's businesses and passions.

In the last eight years that I have been with the team, there were seasons when our members' headcount dropped, and it became challenging to recruit paddlers to fill the gaps. Don't get me wrong, but for the larger part, most participant's priorities change, and time and schedule are always the clinchers. Knowing they have been a part of the team, at least having gone through one major international event, members always come back like family. That familiarity helps them feel welcome in the team.

Besides the interest in the sport, there is the warmth of friendship that enables us to thrive in the team. A real kinship that develops amidst the group despite people's differences. It is not always perfect and each person possesses individual and unique traits and qualities that make them who they are. Good or bad, it is the totality of their personality and character that makes them valuable members and contributors to the team. And especially that not all come from one mold, the differences help compensate for one's lack or the other's strong qualities. The kind of team energy and dynamism that contribute to the rapport of the members.

Given how the team originated and how I got involved in this team from its inception gave me an immediate advantage of being familiar with my fellow members, having started

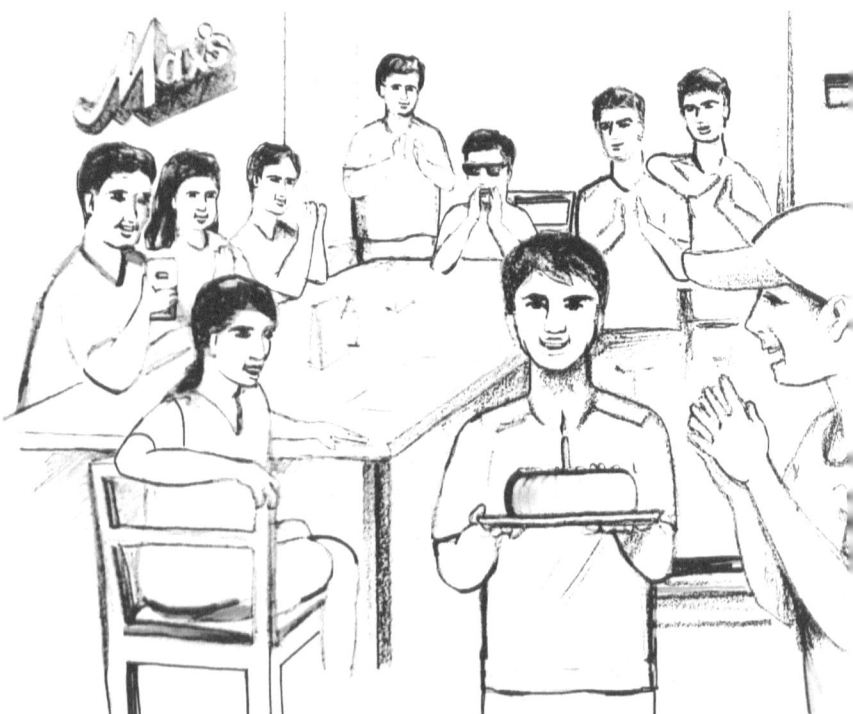

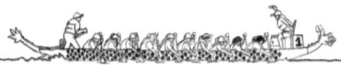

with a small group before we branched out and expanded to friends of friends. Having known them since our college years allowed me to learn and accept them down to their quirks and oddities. That somehow helped strike a balance to keep the team together, having known one another for a long time. We remember each one for their good qualities and detest them for the bad, sometimes ugly, things they bring that sometimes cause issues, or occasionally, difficulties that ensue the inevitable misunderstandings and disagreements or the intricacies of over-familiarity.

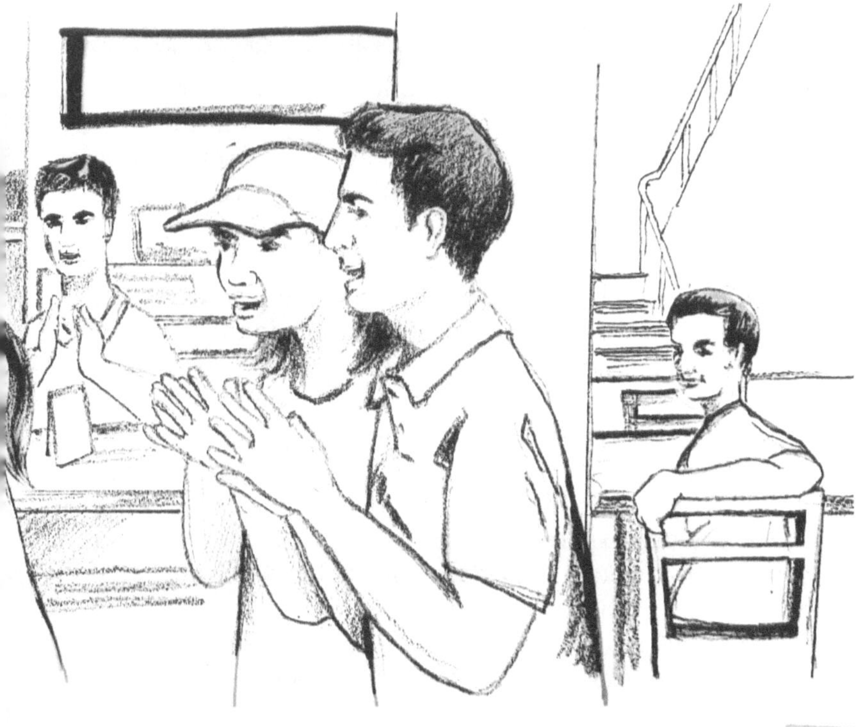

When things like this happen, it can make or break a team. But when they realize and openly settle differences, learn to respect and accept the flaws of one another, it is a wonderful thing. A bond builds and continually shapes and adapts to develop and strengthen the connection among the team. Despite the bad and inevitable, we learn to accept to move on and then learn to live with those flaws and foibles. Once we reach this stage, it is an indicator that the team stands on strong ground. People enjoy each other's company more as they are comfortable being themselves. Much of these efforts are shown through initiatives, simple acts of appreciation, especially from any member who wishes to put the interest of friendship and goodwill front and center.

Take, for example, a fellow team member who fancies arranging training sessions in a novel and unconventional way of training — rowing using a customized audio playlist in place of the usual rigid program sets, an effort done to encourage training even during the off-season. The song is played and we row to the beat of a particular music genre that dates us, and before you know it, we are humming our way down memory lane exchanging stories, one funny story leading to another until we consequently discover how easily we had covered a kilometer's worth of workout. Doing such activity makes our weekend mornings interesting, opens friendly conversation, and adds warmth and novelty to predictable activities.

Our Saturday after-training breakfasts are a staple. This simple effort of getting together benefits more of the newbies since it allows them to get to know the members of the team outside of training. It is also where celebrations take place to acknowledge birthdays, milestones, any reason to whoop it up, and the scope of topics can run from interestingly engaging or hilariously strange. More importantly, it is a chance for all to exchange conversation and be comfortable with each other regardless of age, affiliation, or roots.

During local races, a display of camaraderie is seen when paddlers anticipate the planning of the picnic. When paddlers are more eager to show up first thing in the morning with their potluck, more excited than in the race itself. We regularly get a visit from former members or families of members who simply drop by to support and cheer on the team. Experiencing good times over shared meals and exchanging home-cooked family recipes. There are volunteers who bring whatever they can share, from an assortment of bananas, a large tray of rice cakes, a cooler full of drinks to sharing hammocks, and camp chairs.

Hosting a donation drive for disasters and calamities also helped us express this camaraderie. When news spreads

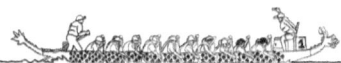

fast and before you know it, you have all your volunteers in one room delegating committees and gathering whatever they can to finish the job. Members want to be involved, quick to offer help and their services, or show up in the assembly for packing and hauling of relief goods. Much of these efforts that lead to camaraderie also continue to occur and be enjoyed off-training.

Going back to my point, the way camaraderie is built is yielded from the intentional efforts of different characters and people who value rapport and team spirit as team virtues. There is a lot more to belonging to a sports team than merely the physical aspect of training we do at the bay or the races we finish. One of the real experiences of being a paddler is the warmth and kinship we gain from these experiences and the relationships and friendships we build along the way that we can keep for a lifetime.

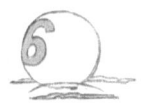

Final Thoughts

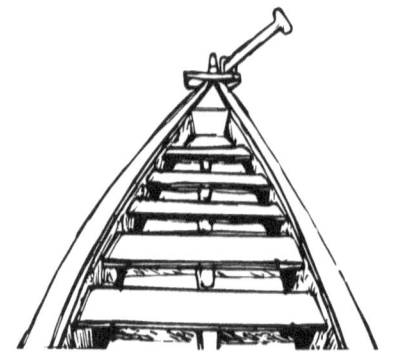

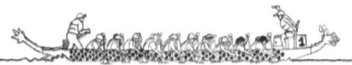

> *"Inaction breeds doubt and fear.*
> *Action breeds confidence and courage.*
> *If you want to conquer fear, do not sit home*
> *and think about it.*
> *Go out and get busy."*
> **Dale Carnegie**

*W*e often breeze through life, living our lives unexpectedly, accepting the circumstances that come our way. We continue to wake up each day, take a shower, drive to work, pay the bills, serve the day's agenda, do the same things again the following day and take a passive acceptance of one's fate. We forget to step back, breathe in the air of experience, and smile to appreciate what life brings us.

It was personally how my eyes saw the world during those years of my dragon boat experience; I lived the days as they happened. I woke up, showed up at the bay, worked my ass off to learn the techniques, prepared well for the races, took the recognition for doing well, drank and partied to reward ourselves, packed up our bags, and headed home to wait for the next event.

Going through that experience and realizing the values I learned in the process teach us that we are all purposed to do something good for one another and for ourselves. Conflict is inevitable in that it lives and breathes around us and arises even more when we do nothing about it. Apparently, the worst enemy is usually ourselves. We normally encounter feelings of doubt, frustration, pride and because we are human, it is convenient to fall into the pits of conflict and give in to our habitual thoughts and emotions.

Seeing through these experiences opened my eyes to the other gains of the sport that never presented itself during those days. And I see the virtues of discipline, punctuality, and respect, determination, perseverance, camaraderie, and teamwork that stood out for me.

Discipline creates that pattern of behavior to keep us within our path and our goals. As an example, it is easy to fall into the comforts of modern daily living, be distracted by our mobile phones, seek attention through social media, listen to gossip, or pay attention to trending issues, but if we train and control our minds to adapt to behavior that keeps us within our objectives, not only helps us get to our goals but also creates meaningful purpose in the things we do.

Punctuality is a byproduct of respect. If we value what we do and integrate the way we manage our time in the things we do, then that behavior tells us that we respect the time we put into the things we value doing. In the same manner, when we show up for an appointment earlier or be readily present on-time, it is a message you are telling that person you appreciate their presence and respect the time they have given you. But then I could say Filipino time is a work in progress. Next!

Determination and perseverance are quite similar, and, in a nutshell, it tells me to never stop paddling! As we navigate through life, we are going to constantly encounter distractions and obstacles along the way. Just like the character of Santiago in Paulo Coelho's The Alchemist, he lost everything midway in pursuit of his Personal Legend. This is cliche, to never give up but hard to live it because we need to realize that the world is not ideal and that we have to accept and take our share in the world's innumerable aspects of discomfort. Okay, maybe to never stop paddling can be a metaphor for now. Constant practice and good habits stretch us to reach new ground.

Professional sports celebrities like Bo Jackson and Kobe Bryant have been quoted for considering camaraderie a significant factor in their respective sports careers and claim to miss it the most, and I can attest to there being nothing that replaces the companionship, trust, and brotherhood one gains from the experiences performing in a team sport. They stay with you long after the fever of the sport has long gone. The good times and sometimes bad experiences are what triggers emotions, perhaps of victory or defeat at the most basic, and of the bittersweet events in and out of the bounds of the sport are what makes of camaraderie. If so, then it is something to nurture and keep. It is the intentional efforts we make, willful

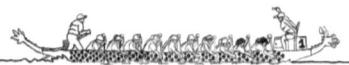

acceptance of differences, and the light, jovial moments that allow us to build friendships along the way.

Finally, teamwork. This value mindset always almost got me out of breath. This one kept me going like the Energizer bunny throughout the races. Every time my mind was telling my body I could not stand it any longer, knowing how hard the team works pushes me further to my limits. If a team works together based on trust, even with a failed outcome, a team can easily spring back to recover. When they work together under a cloud of doubt, even when the goal is achieved, it will not be quite as genuinely fulfilling.

Being middle-aged and living in a world where we can often feel half-hearted about our capabilities, especially in the physical department, and being unable to get out of our comfort zones, can be discouraging. Subjecting ourselves to physical challenges throughout my dragon boat training experience was difficult. Period. Asked if I would do it again, especially after the global pandemic issue is resolved, without missing a heartbeat, definitely. To motivate others through paddling is a privilege. Writing about it is inspiring. Reaching this point and finishing what I wanted to recount makes me even more grateful.

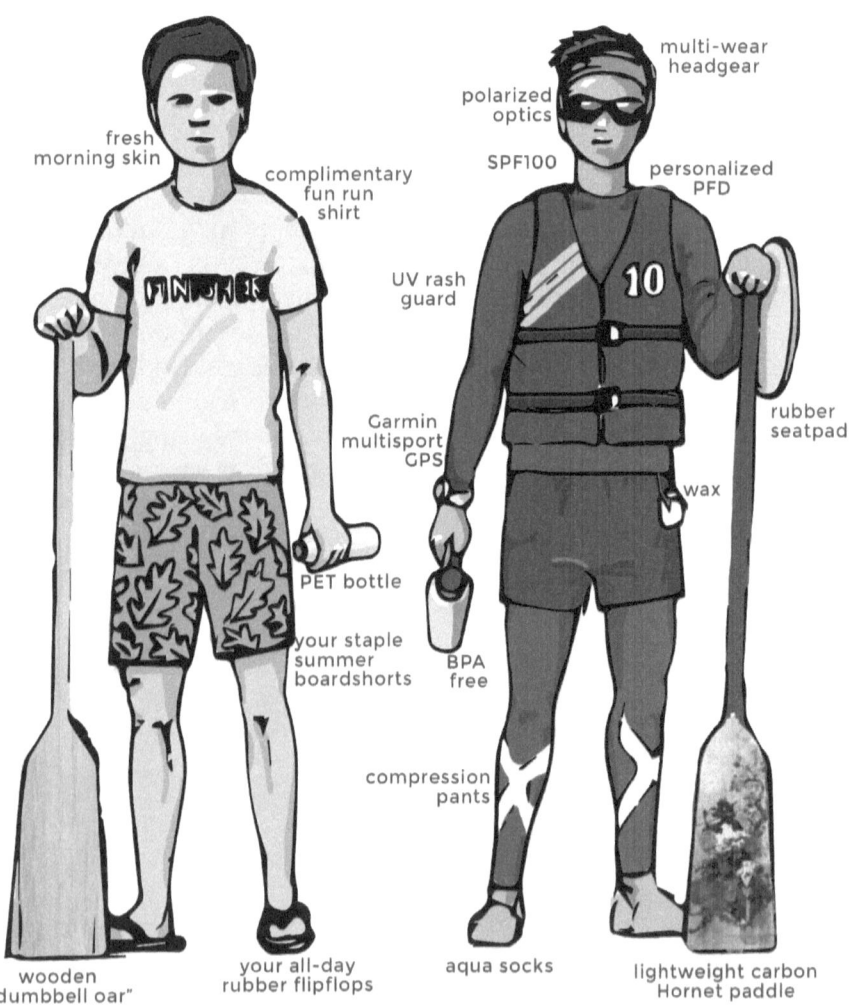

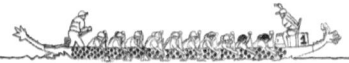

Dragon Boat Glossary and Terms of Basic Commands

Boat parts and positions
1. Bow - Front of boat
2. Stern - Rear of boat
3. Port or Bow side - Left side
4. Starboard or Stroke side - Right side
5. Gunwale (gunnel) - Sides of the boat
6. Pacers or strokes - First paddlers on both sides
7. Till or Tiller - Steersperson and act of steering
8. Cox or coxswain - Steersperson
9. Drummer or signal - A person in front who commands using a drum

Paddle parts
T, Tee or grip - part of the oar held by the inner arm, used in helping push the paddle against the water

Shaft - the long rod that connects the T and the blade

Throat - where the shaft and the blade meet

Blade - the widest part of the paddle

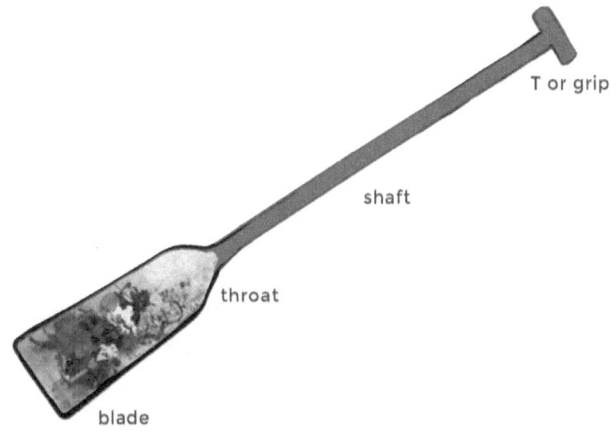

Life In A Boat Shell

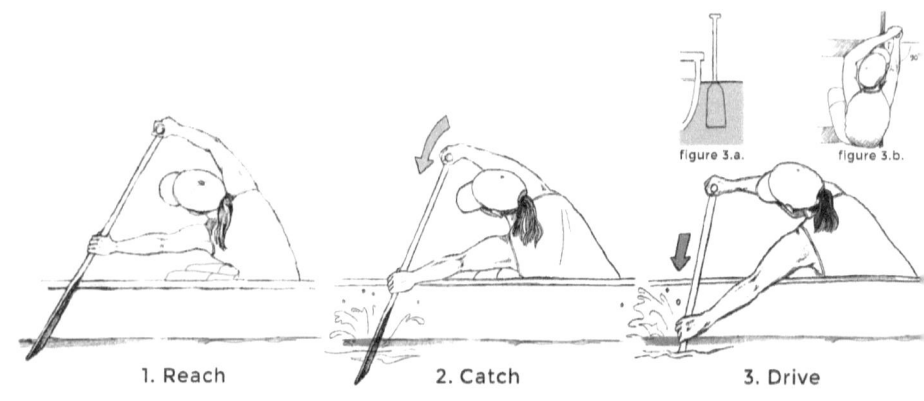

1. Reach   2. Catch   3. Drive

Elements of the stroke/paddling technique

1. Reach - the starting position of the rowing technique also known as the Oars Up position. The length of the stroke is determined in this position. This is basically an extended position where the paddle is a few inches above the water level before driving the boat into the water. In some Asian races, the paddle's blade is already plunged upon this signal, "Are you ready!" which is a part of the next element of the stroke, the catch.

2. Catch - this position begins when the paddle's blade first crushes into the water. Since the goal is to row simultaneously, there is a slight pause in the beginning to help set the timing of the boat. With teamwork and simultaneous coordination, it takes less effort to pull the boat and gain speed. During the catching period, the angle made by the blade should be 45 degrees putting your outside hand/hand in the paddle shaft, under the arm of the person in front of you.

3. Drive - This sets the blade into the water. Once the blade is fully immersed in the water (figure 3.a.), a huge force is required to drive the paddle with both hands, with the bottom arm pulling back the blade and the top arm pushing the T-end to dig with force. Maintain the anchor in such a manner that it will be easy for you to pull it up again. For maximum bite, the angle made by the blade with the side of the boat should be 90 degrees (figure 3.b.)

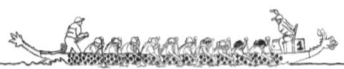

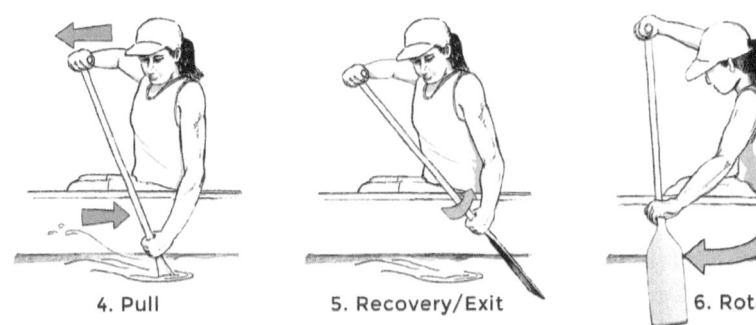

4. Pull   5. Recovery/Exit   6. Rotation

4. Pull - This stroke moves the water, pulling back of the blade parallel to the boat. The top arm stabilizes the paddle whereas the bottom arm and back muscles do the work of pulling back. To impact heavy force, one should rely more upon the back muscles, shoulder and trunk rather than depending upon the arm muscles.

5. Recovery or exit - At the end of the stroke, the exit of the paddle should be done at the hip level. If the stroke goes past the hip, it is considered to be an unnecessary movement and force that can affect the synchrony of the stroke and slow down the boat. To clear the water with the help of the paddle, you should slightly bend your outside arm. In order to aid the process slightly, twist your lower wrist. As soon as the paddle comes out of the water, it is ready to be pushed again. This recovery stage is important because this will help in giving rest to your muscles allowing you to inhale and to regain back your strength.

6. Rotation - this helps in attaining maximum extension and helps a paddler get an extra 2-4 inches with every stroke. On an average count, if 20 people will impose the rotational force simultaneously then it can add up to 7 feet to the stroke. This rotational force is done in a smooth and elastic manner.

Source: https://www.tutorialspoint.com/dragon_boating/dragon_boating_stroke_techniques.htm

Common boat commands and terms

ALL BOATS HOLD Starter referee's call signifying that he/she is getting alignment of all boats. Be ready and focus on your team only to respond, the race is starting any second.

ATTENTION! Your steerer's command to get into READY!

READY! position. This term is used to indicate that the race is about to begin in a few seconds!

OARS ON THE SIDE or ALL DOWN! Command from drummer/steersperson to stop paddling and rest with paddles on laps.

BACK PADDLING The stroke used to bring a boat backward into or away from a dock or a race start.

HOLD THE BOAT or BRACE THE BOAT or FLARE THE BOAT To stabilize the boat. Paddle blades flat on the surface of the water with blades gently feathering back and forth with a slight downward pressure to stabilize the boat. The shaft of the paddle pressed against the top of the gunwales. Used especially when transferring seat positions or a wake is coming in broadside. This command will steady the boat from rocking side to side.

DRUMMER The person who sets a crew's timing by rhythmically pounding a drum or calling stroke rates. The drummer sits in the bow and is usually lightweight.

FLAGCATCHER The person responsible for catching the flag. If the flag is not pulled and held for at least 1 sec or thereabouts, then the flag is not considered caught.

LOAD THE BOAT Step onto the boats after having put on and buckled your PFD, with everything ready to go. When getting on the boat, be sure to do so one person at a time, one foot at a time. Start by stepping as close to the middle of the boat as possible, and once both feet are in, keep your profile low --in effect, lower the center of gravity. NOTE: Load from the back seat to the front seat.

PFD Personal Floatation Device (please do not refer to them

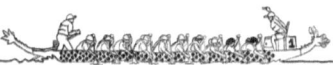

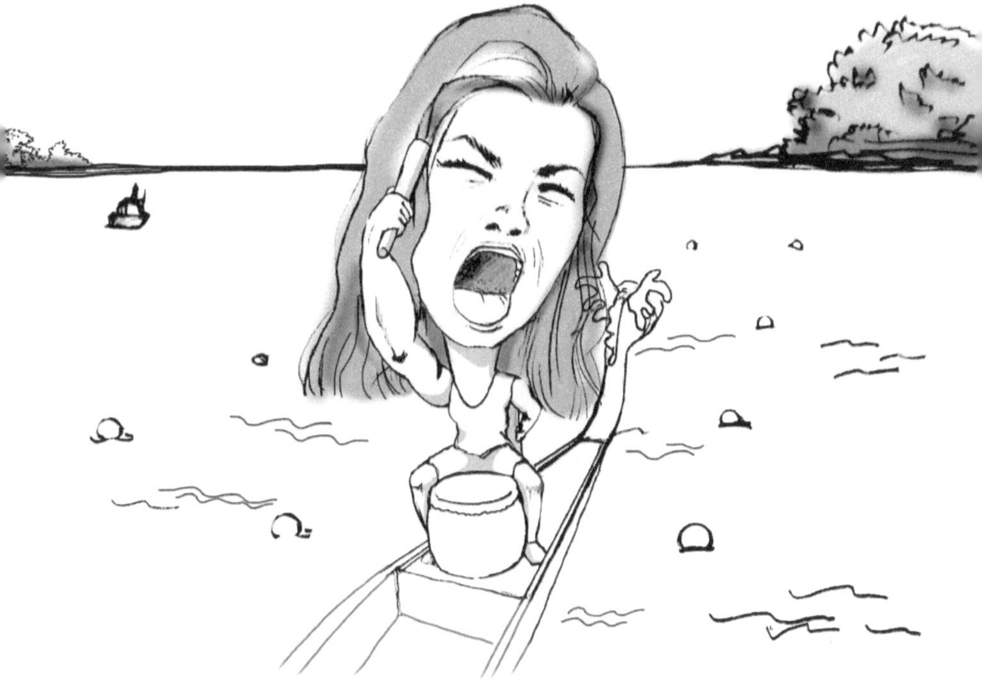

as life vests). A Coast Guard approved PFD will be required to be worn by each person on the boat for their own personal safety.

OARS UP or PADDLES UP! Get ready to paddle. Paddles are poised above the water ready to take a stroke. Commonly used for starting the movement of the boat in a non-race situation. The paddles are paused in the catch position until the command to start paddling is given. Paddles in prep or recovery position / 5 inches off the water and 1 inch away from the boat

STARTS The first strokes usually in counts from 10-50 in a race or a race program that helps accelerate, pick up the speed and pull the boat forward

LONGS These are the strokes in the middle of the program where the reach and rotation are maximized and fully extended. The drummer or steersman prepares the signal by call-

Life In A Boat Shell

ing READY FOR LONGS! A command to signal paddlers for a longer reach for a more effective recovery

PICK UP! A command to tell the paddlers to increase the speed/tempo of their stroke. Very important not to push the team's stroke rate up to the point it starts to lose sync. Also very important to project your voice to the paddlers at the front of the boat so they bring the stroke rate up or you may find the back of the boat rushing the stroke causing the team to lose synchronization and power.

READY FOR LAST KICK! This set of strokes occurs towards the finish line in a race. The drummer calls out this signal to prepare the paddlers to put in more power in this set of strokes until the finish line. The drummer's timing is critical as he/she is tasked to estimate the ability of the paddlers' remaining power to effectively pull the boat faster, the position of the contenders in a race and the remaining distance to the finish line.

Source:: http://dragonboathawaii.com/docs/glossary.pdf

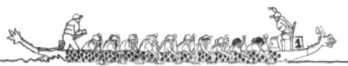

Acknowledgments

It all started with a sketch pad, a few books to read and many moments of staying home during the months of the Covid19 lockdown. This composition of thoughts could not have been possible until I started to appreciate the opportune time in my hands. Many of these insights were alive again after much reading and listening to podcasts.

While the accounts and the experiences are first-hand, there is nothing new with the insights and wisdom that I have shared since this wisdom is already out there, being taught, practiced, and personified by people, many of whom live among us and may already be applying it in the real world and our day-to-day lives.

None of this would have been possible if not for my dear friend and most enthusiastic supporter, Dale. After much coaxing and many iterations, it had led me to finish something I could not have imagined. From my early drafts and him repeatedly reminding me to finish what I start, to giving meaningful advice and sharing his opinion on the layout, he was always ready to help.

To my daughter, Yvonne for patiently answering my random questions during the early weeks trying to learn the tools for digitizing my pencil illustrations.

To my dragon boat team whom I have made memories with, thank you for the experiences and the inspiration that continue to help foster a lifelong friendship.

Finally to my family and close friends who never had a clue what occupied me for the larger part of the lockdown, the video calls, chats and shared virtual moments helped me appreciate the simple things in life even more.

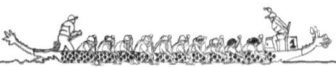

About the Author

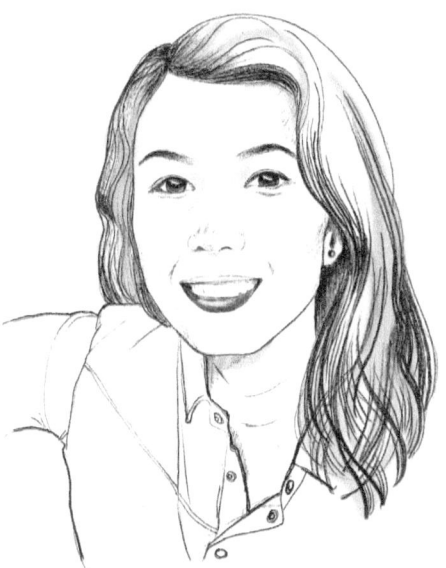

Pinky Manzano has had a passion for arts and design since she won her first on-the-spot art contest at the age of five, which subsequently led her to develop and earn her Bachelor's Degree in Fine Arts from the University of Santo Tomas, starting out professionally as a graphics artist. Outside her brand marketing and retail merchandising practice, she dabbles in journaling, illustrating, and digital graphic design. Her eight years of paddling experience in local and international racing events prepared her to write essays about dragon boat.

www.ingramcontent.com/pod-product-compliance
Lightning Source LLC
Chambersburg PA
CBHW030507220526
45464CB00006B/2701